Summer Visits

to

Buckhead, Georgia

and

Swords, Georgia

By
John W. Wright

2005
Parkway Publishers, Inc.
Boone, North Carolina

Copyright ©2005 by John W. Wright

All Rights Reserved

Library of Congress Cataloging-in-Publication Data

Wright, John W.
  Summer visits to Buckhead, Georgia and Swords, Georgia / by John W. Wright.
      p. cm.
   ISBN 1-887905-43-X
   1. Wright, John W.--Childhood and youth. 2. Wright, John W.--Family. 3. Buckhead (Morgan County, Ga.)--Biography. 4. Swords (Ga.)--Biography. 5. Summer--Georgia--Buckhead (Morgan County) 6. Summer--Georgia--Swords. 7. Buckhead (Morgan County, Ga.)--Social life and customs--20th century. 8. Swords (Ga.)--Social life and customs--20th century. I. Title.

   F294.B926W75 2005
   975.8'595'092--dc22

2004021348

Typeset and Cover Design by: Beth Jacquot

"Papa" John W. Wright
with
Peyton and Tanner

To
Peyton Wright Bothur
and
Tanner Wright Bothur

who brought a glow to
my golden years

The ancients used to say that all roads lead to Rome, but I say all roads lead to Buckhead and Swords. You can go anywhere in the Western Hemisphere – anywhere – from the Strait of Magellan at the bottom of South America to the top of Alaska and find a road that will get you to Buckhead and Swords. But there is not one single road, not a single one in all the Western Hemisphere that will get you to Rome – now, just think about that!!

Contents

Foreword ix
Acknowlegments xiii
Buckhead
    Grandma Said 15
    Sam, Dixie and Peggy 17
    Sugar Creek 21
    Mendacity 25
    A Moment Remembered 29
    Genuine Relief 33
    Just Plain Stuck 37
    Puttin' Me On 41
    Seeing Hearing and Remembering 43

Swords
    The Day We Buried Lula May 65
    Downright Mortified 73
    Growing Up 77
    Take It to the Cows in Prayer 81
    I'll Fly Away 83
    Lord Have Mercy on My Soul 85
    Between a Rock and a Hard Place 89
    Tramps, Hobos and The Swords Depot 93
    The Swords General Store 97
    A Pain in the Ass 105
    Decided Opinions 109

Foreword

My grandchildren were born at the very dawn of the twenty first century. They were born into a science-based megatechnic, urban culture in which they will witness further space exploration along with the continuing magnification of power and speed. Theirs will be a global world – a world of jets, television, computers, the internet and cell phones – an increasingly digitized world in which their experience of reality will depend more and more upon its being representable as numbers. They will be members of the "nanosecond generation", if you will.

By way of contrast, the individuals in my short stories were all born in the nineteenth century – one as early as 1859, and two at the conclusion of the American Civil War. They grew up in the waning moments in western civilization of a slower, more locally-oriented agrarian culture – a form of culture that many still living recall through their memory of grandparents and great-grandparents, whose style of life and values were formed by the remaining traces of this earlier era. In time, my ancestors would experience the transforming effects of rural electrification, refrigeration, the telephone, indoor plumbing and the motorcar, but that would come in their later years.

In contrast to my adult experience in the cosmopolitan atmosphere of a large northeastern research-oriented university, I retain vivid memories from childhood of fields being turned by mule drawn plows, cotton being picked by "field hands," the sounds of the local blacksmith's hammer and of horse-drawn wagons tied up to the poles supporting the corrugated tin roof extending from the front of the Swords General Store.

As a youngster, my summer visits in the 1930s and early 40s to the rural Morgan County communities of Buckhead and Swords, Georgia, provided memories that have greatly enriched my life. It is against this background that I have attempted to share with my grandchildren's generation something of the flavor of times past, but not forgotten.

Although separated by some three miles, Buckhead and Swords had been united for me through the marriage of my parents. My mother, Mildred Elizabeth Bond, was from Swords and my father, John Walter Wright, from Buckhead. Typically, over the course of my visits, I would alternate back and forth, staying with the Wrights in Buckhead for about a week, then migrating down to Swords where I would spend a similar amount of time with the Bond, Cochran and Swords families on my mother's side. For a city kid, born in Wilmington, North Carolina, my visits to rural Georgia were happy, carefree times, close to nature and filled with enchanting new discoveries. Perhaps, even more enduring, they were occasions in which I was exposed to such values as self-denial, fidelity, honesty, thrift and stewardship – values inherent to individuals who had lived in their communities over long periods of time, were close to the land and whose lives had been shaped by the disciplined requisites of the high and honorable calling of farming.

As a grandchild, my visits with "Walt" and "Fannie" Wright in Buckhead had a down-to-earth quality. For a youngster from the city, theirs was a different world; one of cows to be milked, milk to be churned, hogs to be slopped, vegetables to be gathered from the garden, corn to be shucked, wood to be chopped and fields to be plowed, all by hand. A world of featherbeds, fireplaces, coal oil lamps, ice boxes, large black cast-iron cooking stoves, privies, barns and farm animals; of water drawn from a well, baths taken in nearby Sugar Creek and weekly trips to a fish camp on the Apalachee River to check the trotlines for catfish – a warm, personal world, characterized by a sense of daily routine and accountability.

The Swords community, on the other hand, presented a somewhat different set of circumstances. Whereas my grandparents on the Wright side in Buckhead were solid middle-class people, my mother's relatives, the Bonds, Cochrans and Swords not only formed an extended family, but also one possessed of considerable wealth. In the early 1890's my great-grandfather, John Buchanon Swords began purchasing land in what had previously been known as the Blue Springs area. By 1900, he had amassed a farm consisting of some three thousand acres. Beyond the farm, John "Buck" Swords literally built himself a town, which was incorporated in 1906 and named Swords.

Swords' son-in-law, John Hill Cochran, managed the Swords Supply Company (later known as the Swords

General Store) and was the Swords depot agent for the Georgia Railroad. Another son-in-law, Emory Allen Bond, ran the gristmill and his wife, Lula May Swords Bond, served as the Swords postmistress. John "Buck", in addition to being President of the Swords Bank, ran the Swords Distillery and the Swords cotton gin. He was also active in politics, having been a member of the county Democratic Executive Committee, elected to the Georgia State House of Representatives in 1916, and in 1919 elected a County Commissioner. Each of the families had impressive homes, as well as extensive farming, livestock and timber interests. I think that it is not unreasonable to suggest that prior to the invasion of the boll weevil in 1921, at which time cotton was dethroned as "king", Swords was as close to an antebellum plantation as one was likely to find after the Civil War. However, from my perspective as a child, and more often than not, to the dismay of the family, I had the "run" of the whole place in a way that I did not have in Buckhead.

In their own distinctive ways, both communities, Buckhead and Swords, provide the setting for the following childhood recollections.

Acknowledgements

Life's undertakings are made easier with the aid of friends. With that in mind, I want to express my appreciation for the generosity of Carol Cross, Ethel Atkinson, Grayson White and the late Martha McWhorter Nunnally who in various ways helped me refresh my childhood memories of Buckhead and Swords.

Until the last decades of the eighteenth century, the Apalachee and Oconee Rivers constituted the boundary separating the Creek Indians to the West and the newly arriving settlers to the East. Little was known about lands to the West. In 1795, however, an individual by the name of Booth Fitzpatrick crossed the Apalachee River into what is now known as Morgan County. Later, that same year, he returned with several companions to the branch where he had made camp on his earlier foray. There, they killed a large buck deer and fastened his head to a white oak tree near the spring. In 1807 when Morgan County was formed, the district in which the spring was located was called the Buckhead district. Buckhead acquired its first post office in 1823. Later, in 1837, when the railroad came through, the Georgia Railroad designated its depot as "Buckhead, Georgia". The Fitzpatrick family cemetery can still be found in the area.

The Civil War affected Buckhead. The Buckhead historical marker, which was erected by the Georgia Historical Commission, states:

> On November 19, 1864, Federal troops under General Geary, Sherman's 20th Army Corp drove a small detachment of Confederate soldiers out of Buckhead, ate dinner and then destroyed the water tank, all railroad buildings and a large supply of cordwood. Moving out of Buckhead, the Federals destroyed the railroad to the Oconee

River, there burning the bridge and railroad supplies....

The post Civil War years cast a dark cloud over many small southern communities. "The lost cause" had separated families and cost the lives of its young men. Invading armies had left scorched fields. The destruction of railroad beds and bridges resulted in the collapse of their transportation systems. Notwithstanding these and other difficulties, by 1891, Buckhead had become an incorporated town and, by the turn of the century, it was on its way to becoming a prosperous community. The Empire Cotton Oil Company was founded in 1898. The town had a cotton gin and a cotton buyers' office, reflecting the fact that cotton was "king." By 1900, both Baptist and Methodist Churches were well established. Buckhead had its own Masonic Hall. There were four general merchandise stores, a saw and planing mill, a fertilizer plant, an ax and hoe handle factory, two blacksmith shops, two livery stables and the Sunnyside Hotel provided a place for "drummers" and railroad crews to stay.

By the beginning of World War II, however, many of the conditions that had led to Buckhead's earlier prosperity were no longer in place. Momentum continued to shift from the "local" to more distant "urban" centers. The arrival of the boll weevil in 1921 had the effect of dethroning cotton as "king," thereby further undermining the local economy. If these factors were not enough, the stock market crash of 1929 and the ensuing depression years, brought added difficulties.

Today, although a quieter place, Buckhead retains much of its earlier charm.

(The author gratefully acknowledges that the information presented in this chapter is based on conversations with the late Mrs. Martha McWhorter Nunnally of Buckhead.)

"Papa"
James Walter Wright
1866-1951

"Grandma"
Mary Frances Robins Wright
1865-1949

They were affectionately known as "Walt" and "Fannie." Walt was born in the southern part of Greene County, Georgia, near the Walker Methodist Church. Fannie was born during the last year of the Civil War in the community of Harmony in Putnam County, Georgia. They were married in 1889 and had three children: Sara Lee (1892-1968), Seals Robins (1897-1977) and the author's father, John Walter (1899-1981). Beginning in 1899, Walt and Fannie lived most of their adult lives in the community of Buckhead, Georgia, prior to moving to Atlanta where they lived with their daughter in their late years. While living in Buckhead, Walt farmed, cut and milled timber, had a livery stable, bought and sold livestock and drove a school bus. They were active in the Buckhead Methodist Church where Walt had been a member of the

Building Committee when the church was rebuilt in 1915 and Fannie had been a charter member of the Women's Society of Christian Service. Fannie enjoyed working in her garden and flowerbeds and Walt liked to "coon" hunt and fish at his camp on the Apalachee River. They are buried in Westview Cemetery in Atlanta along with two of their children, Sara Lee and Seals. The photograph of "Walt" was taken circa 1910. The photograph of "Fannie" was taken in 1936.

"Grandma" Mary Frances Robins Wright with her children: Sara Lee (1892-1968); the author's father, John Walter (1899-1981); and Seals Robins (1897-1977)

Photograph circa 1900.

"Walt" and "Fannie" Wright lived in this late 19th century house from 1899 until 1945 when they moved to Atlanta to live with their daughter. The house was located in Buckhead on the Swords-Parks Mill Road near its intersection with Saffold Road. The house was torn down circa 2002.

The Home of James Walter Wright and Mary Frances Robins Wright

"Uncle Seals"
Seals Robins Wright
1897-1977

Photograph taken circa 1920.

Seals Robins Wright was born in Greene County, Georgia. In 1899, he moved with his parents to the community of Buckhead where he lived with them throughout his life, assisting with various chores on the farm. During the 1930's and '40's he drove a school bus, the route of which included Buckhead, Swords, Parks Mill and other parts of southeast Morgan County. Seals' interests included bird hunting and checking his trotlines for catfish at his and his father's fish camp on the Apalachee River. Seals never married. He is buried beside his parents and sister in Westview Cemetery in Atlanta, Georgia.

"Walt" Wright with his dogs,
Left to right, Dixie, Peggy and Sam

Photograph taken in 1939.

*"Walt" Wright at his home in Buckhead:
Drawing Water from the Well and
Churning Milk on the Back Porch*

Photographs circa 1938.

***"Walt" and Seals Wright's Fish Camp
on the Apalachee River***

Photograph circa 1938

The Old Oak Tree in Grandma Wright's Pasture

Grandma Said

It was always a kind of mystery to me why Grandma kept a bucket by her kitchen door.

So, one day I asked her.

"Why?"

I always had lots of questions and most of them began and ended with "why" and "how." Grandma said that the bucket was there so she could have a place to collect her old grease, suet and pieces of "taller."

Well, naturally I had to ask.

"Why?"

"To make soap with," she said.

"Why?"

"To wash clothes and little boys with, to keep them looking like new."

At that point my question shifted.

"How? – How do you make soap?"

"Well," Grandma said, "first, you build a fire under an iron wash pot and then you pour your grease into the pot. I like hog grease myself, but most any kind will do. Then you add the lye. In the old days we made our own lye by saving the ashes from the fireplace and dripping water over the ashes and collecting the water after it had passed through the ashes." Grandma said, "I like hickory wood ashes best, but you could make lye from most any kind of ashes." Grandma said, "Nowadays I use 'store bought' Red Devil lye, but whichever way you do it, the old way or the new way, you still use about two pounds of grease to a gallon of lye. Then you bring it to a boil and stir it for a long time."

"Why?"

"So it will thicken up good and then you pour it into a shallow cake pan."

"Why?"

"So it will get hard over night and you can cut it into little blocks in the morning." Grandma said that sometimes she put perfume in the soap to make it "pretty," but that I was pretty enough as I was, so she didn't see any need to put perfume in my soap. Anyway she said, I'd about "whyed?" and "howed?" her to death for one day and that I should run along and play.

That's what my grandma said, so that's what I did!

Sam, Dixie and Peggy

Have you ever wondered what a dog has on his mind? I mean, have you ever wondered what a dog is thinking about? Papa said that "you could tell how intelligent a dog was by how long it took you to figure out what he was thinking." But my problem was that I could never quite figure out what a dog was thinking in the first place which seemed to suggest that the dog was either pretty intelligent or that I was pretty dumb or something like that.

One day, about twenty minutes to noon, when Papa and I were sitting on the front porch, Papa turned to me and said, "John Walter, keep your eye on the corner of the house and see if Sam, Dixie and Peggy don't come walking out toward the dirt road in front of the house." Sam, Dixie and Peggy were Papa and Uncle Seals' dogs. Sam was an old bird dog, Dixie was a young bird dog and Peggy was a Boston Bull Terrier, the only "Yankee" in the bunch. Well, sure enough, in about a minute, Sam, Dixie and Peggy came walking single file around the corner of the house – Sam first, then Dixie with Peggy bringing up the rear – they walked slowly across the front yard and sat down beside the dirt road across from the railroad tracks.

Usually, Sam, Dixie and Peggy just laid around the backyard not doing much of anything, but every day about twenty minutes to noon, here would come Sam, Dixie and Peggy, just taking their time and always walking one behind the other – always with Sam in front, Dixie in the middle and Peggy bringing up the rear. Every day, even on Sunday when the Lord said dogs could rest – every day – you could set your clock by it – at twenty minutes to noon Sam, Dixie, and Peggy would slowly make their way across the front yard to the edge of the road and proceed to sit down beside each other.

Papa knew a lot about dogs. You might say that he was a kind of "dogologist." So when I asked Papa what was going on, he said, "Dogs not only have better noses for smelling than people but they can also hear better. What is going on is that when the midday train blows its whistle about ten miles away for the Oconee River crossing, the dogs can hear the whistle even though we can't." Papa said that it made the dogs feel good to sit beside the road and howl as the train pulled into Buckhead. He said if you watch what a dog does you can usually figure out what he's thinking.

Anyway, Papa said that just because we couldn't hear the train whistle blow ten miles away when it comes to the river crossing doesn't mean that the dogs can't hear it – and when they hear it they began having a little discussion among themselves, you know. Sam probably said, "I think I hear the train whistle," and Peggy probably said, "Well, what are we waiting for?" or something like that. So, they all got up, shook themselves and made their way to the side of the road.

So, there they were, Sam, Dixie and Peggy patiently sitting beside each other next to the road waiting for the train to arrive – they knew it would come because it always did. Papa said, "they knew it was coming because they could hear the train whistle blow for Swords, about three miles down the road – two long blows, one short blow and then another long blow.

Sure enough, in about five minutes the train arrived in Buckhead. It was huffing and a puffing, steam shooting out of its pistons as it blew its whistle for the Buckhead crossing – and Sam, Dixie and Peggy were howling away in full voice – giving it everything they had!! They kept howling until the train came to a stop and had quieted down and then they quieted down – but they didn't move because they knew that they would get another chance to howl when the train pulled out of town – so, they just sat there and waited while the mail was unloaded and the passengers boarded the train. Then slowly, as the train began to pull out of the station – huffing and a puffing – Sam, Dixie and Peggy once again began howling at the top of their lungs. When the train was out of sight and they could no longer hear it, they got up and with Sam taking the lead, Dixie following and Peggy bringing up the rear, three happy and contented dogs slowly made their way to the backyard to await another day and one more chance to do their thing.

Sugar Creek

It was Saturday again, the day before church, which meant that bath-taking time had rolled around once more. We always took a bath once a week whether we needed it or not. I never was too big on soap and taking a bath. Early on, I discovered that a little dust didn't keep me awake at night and that Grandma's cooking tasted just as good when I was dirty as when I was clean.

On the other hand, taking a bath with Papa and Uncle Seals was different. In fact, it had its enjoyable side in spite of soap and things like that. For one thing, it gave me a chance to ride in Uncle Seals' school bus. Uncle Seals drove a school bus and we went everywhere in the school bus – to church, to the fish camp on the Apalachee River, even to take a bath down on Sugar Creek. Uncle Seals' school bus was like having the biggest car in the neighborhood.

When it was 'bout time, Papa would say, "John Walter, go sweep out the bus and then we'll head down to Sugar Creek and wash-up for Sunday." So, I'd go sweep out the bus and pretty soon we'd be on our way. Uncle Seals would drive and Papa would sit up front on a bench near Seals. Uncle Seals' school bus didn't have seats like they do today – it had a long bench running down each side and one down the middle.

For some reason I never quite understood, we never took Grandma with us, but we always took all the dogs: Sam, Dixie, and Peggy. So, we were off to Sugar Creek – Papa, Uncle Seals, me, two southern dogs, and Peggy, the Bostonian. Some of the local people said that, as we passed through the community of Buckhead, we "looked like Noah's Ark on wheels, what with three dogs and John Walter hanging out the school bus windows."

Papa and Uncle Seals knew a good washing place when they saw one. So, we made our way to our secret washing place down on Sugar Creek. Sugar Creek was a few miles south of Buckhead. You had to go down a winding dirt road through the woods in order to get there. It was Papa and Seals' favorite place to take a bath because it had a good tree to hang our clothes on and the rocks in the Creek were good for sitting on while we washed-up and talked. Sometimes we would just sit there for almost two hours and talk. There was always lots to talk about – what chores needed to be taken care of, when we would go down to the fish camp and check the trotlines for catfish and other things that needed to be done. Once Papa and Seals got situated on their favorite rock, the first thing they did was to use some of Grandma's homemade soap to lather-up the dogs. We washed the dogs first so they could shake and dry off before we headed home. Then we would leisurely wash ourselves. It was a sight to behold, two grown men, me, and three dogs – and none of us had a stitch of clothes on. Papa said that being naked didn't seem to bother the dogs and he "sho" wasn't going to let it bother him.

Well, we made our way home, all bright and shiny. Sitting in church the next day, I wasn't too sure how my inside looked to God, but at least my outside was pretty clean!

Mendacity

When I was a kid I was a little rough around the edges – at least that was the thinking of my Uncle Seals and nobody seemed to disagree with him. So, Uncle Seals set out to do what he could to smooth my edges and polish me up in hopes of making me a bit more presentable to the world.

One way Seals went about shaping me up was to introduce me to new words and on this particular day the word he chose was "mendacity." As he was wont to do from time to time, he sat me down and asked me if I was acquainted with the word, mendacity. I said, "No, I don't think I'm acquainted with that word." Seals explained that mendacity didn't exactly mean outright lying, but had to do with exaggerating or stretching the truth – that people who made a habit of stretching the truth were thought to be mendacious. Then Seals asked if I got the drift of what he was saying, and I said, "Yeah, I think so." Then he asked, "Now, you wouldn't want people to think of you as being mendacious, would you?" and I said, "Heck no."

Now, you have to understand that Uncle Seals never started these discussions out of the blue. They always followed something that had already happened and that's what I want to tell you about, what happened the day before we had our discussion about mendacity. You see, the day before we had our talk, me and Seals took the school bus and headed down to his fish camp on the Apalachee River to check the trotlines for catfish. When we got there, we took Seal's bateau (flat bottomed boat with blunt ends) and poled our way up river to where the trotlines were strung out across the river. Then we began unhooking the catfish. We had unhooked a pretty good mess of fish when Seals noticed something strange on the trotline, like nothing he had ever seen before. When Seals pulled it out of the water, it nigh on scared me to death! It had big flat scales and a head like an alligator. It was about the meanest looking thing I'd ever seen. Seals said it was an alligator garfish, the only one he'd ever caught.

As we were heading back to Buckhead, Seals said that we ought to take the garfish down town and show it to everybody, so, that's what we did. We made out for John Jacob's General Store in the middle of Buckhead. Holding the garfish, I soon found myself surrounded by people. One man said, "That's the ugliest thing I've ever seen!" Someone else said, "Lord, that is one terrible looking fish!" About that time, a farmer wearing bib overalls stepped forward and asked, "John Walter, how long would you say that fish is?" I said, " I reckon it's about ten feet long!"

Later, as me and Uncle Seals were walking up the dirt road toward Grandma and Grandpa Wright's house, Seals said, "John Walter, don't you think you stretched the length of that fish a little too much? That fish wasn't over three and one half feet if it was an inch. If you'd stretched that fish any longer, it would have broken in two right in front of everybody!" Then Seals mumbled something about mendacity, but it wasn't until the next day that he sat me down and talked to me about mendacity and being mendacious.

Well, I want to tell you, my discussion with Uncle Seals about mendacity was real bothersome. For several days I thought hard about it. The thought of being infected with mendacity sounded worse than having measles or even chicken pox. In fact, it weighed so heavy on my mind that I finally turned to Grandma in hopes of getting some relief.

Grandma said that she didn't think I was mendacious, but that I had come pretty close – that if I'd added another inch to the length of that garfish I would probably have crossed the mendacity line. As I was about to leave, Grandma said, "You sure have grown a lot since last summer. How tall are you now?" I said, "I reckon I'm about ten feet tall!"

A Moment Remembered

My Grandma Wright, "Fannie," was a tall, graceful woman. I remember the quiet satisfaction she derived from leisurely combing her long reddish hair, which she would roll and wear in a bun, a kind of therapeutic ritual undertaken at the beginning of each day. I also remember her as a very gentle person who went about her daily chores in an unhurried manner – taking pleasure in her rather informal flower beds – who, following each meal, would spread a linen cloth over the remaining food, always leaving a supply of freshly baked half-moon peach pies for my indulgence between meals. But, most of all, I remember the gentle, yet effective ways in which she taught me about life.

One morning, Grandma was about her daily chores and I was trailing her everywhere she went – underfoot, so to speak, and in a grumpy mood. This had gone wrong and that had gone wrong and life just wasn't worth living. Grandma continued on with her work, but after a while she stopped, put my hand in hers and asked softly, "Would you like to take a little walk with me?" So, hand in hand, we walked out the back door, past the hen house, past the privy and beyond the barn to the pasture and on a way till we came to a wooden bench and there we sat side by side. Being a little confused, I asked Grandma, "Why are we doing this? Why have we come out here just to sit on the bench together?"

Grandma didn't answer my question directly, but pointed to a craggy, old oak tree standing all by itself in the middle of the pasture and said, "Do you see that tree?" and I said, "Yeah, Grandma."

Then, Grandma said, "Sometimes when I'm feeling grumpy and out of sorts, I come down to the pasture and sit on my little bench and talk to the tree, and you know, sometimes the tree speaks to me." I said, "What do you mean, Grandma? What does the tree say to you?"

"Well," she said, "for one thing, it kinda smiles at me and says, 'I'm very, very old and I've lived through lots of rainy days and cold snowy days, even thunder storms.'"

"What else does the tree say, Grandma?"

"Sometimes the tree points to that crooked limb, the one with the big bend in it, that kinda turns down and then turns back up – the old tree told me, that when it was very young, the wind blew a nearby tree over that limb and it just laid there for about twenty years. And then it smiled again and said, 'sometimes you need to help your neighbor.'"

"What else did the old tree say, Grandma?" Then Grandma told me how lightning had destroyed the top of the old tree and left it with a scar that ran all the way down the side of its trunk – "But most of all," Grandma said, "I like the old tree's spirit, how it just keeps on smiling and refuses to let life's problems get it down."

Sometimes it takes a long time for the deeper meaning of things to come through. I often think about me and Grandma sitting in the pasture together talking to that old tree. In fact, when I'm in that neck of the woods, I always stop and visit the old tree. It's still there – smiling – the wind blowing through its leaves, as if to say, "Life is good, live it!"

Genuine Relief

If you went out the back door and down the back steps of Grandma and Grandpa Wright's house, you came face-to-face with one of the best used paths in the whole state of Georgia – and if you decided to walk down the path, you would eventually come to a little house. The little house had an opening that allowed you to go inside, but it didn't have a door that you could open and shut. A few feet in front of the opening, there was a lattice frame that was completely covered by a sweet smelling wisteria vine with blue and purple blossoms. So, if you wanted to go inside the little house, you had to walk around the wisteria vine. An interesting thing was, that once you were inside, you could look out the opening and through the sweet smelling wisteria vine and see everything that was going on outside but nobody on the outside could see through the vine and know what you were up to on the inside! For that reason, the little house was called a privy, which was just a fancy way of saying that it was a private place. Now, Webster's dictionary says a privy is "a small building with a bench with holes through which the user may evacuate," whatever that means.

My Uncle Seals said a privy was a pretty "Holy" place, and he was right. It was a holey place all right! It had a big hole, a smaller hole, and a little hole – a kinda Papa Bear, Mama

Bear and Baby Bear hole! But, for some reason, it was next to impossible to get anybody to give you a straight answer as to what a privy was used for. When I asked Uncle Seals, he just said, "If you want eggs, you go to the hen house; if you want vegetables you go to the vegetable garden, if you want to be close to God, you go to church, but, if you want "genuine relief," you head for the privy!" Well, it took a while, but I eventually got the message!

There's no question about it, the privy did have a way of drawing people to it – a kind of natural attraction I'd say. At least once a day we all paid a visit to the privy to get our share of "genuine relief" even though nobody was ever very up-front as to why they went. Papa had his own way of announcing his need to visit the privy. He could have been talking with anybody, a neighbor, the preacher, or the Queen of England – if he needed some "genuine relief" he'd say, "I need to go see a man about a horse."

As you know, life has its unpleasant as well as its more pleasant aspects. On the unpleasant side of things, the privy didn't always have the most pleasant aroma – especially if the wind was from the wrong direction – even though the sweet smelling wisteria vine did help! On the other hand, when I was doing my thing in the privy, I was "as relaxed as a dead pig in the sunshine," for not only did the privy provide "genuine relief," it also provided a Sears & Roebuck catalogue – and as everybody knows, the Sears & Roebuck catalogue had more than one use! Since we didn't have toilet paper like we have today, I would just rip a page out of the catalogue and tidy myself up a little bit.

But even after I ripped a few pages out, there was always at least three hundred pages left to look at, and on each page there were "good," "better," and "best" pictures. The Sears & Roebuck catalogue had a picture of everything in the whole wide world in it no matter whether it was Bibles, shoes or bicycles, there was always a picture of a "good" bicycle, a "better" bicycle and the "best" bicycle. Naturally, you had to take a close look at each picture in order to see what made something "good," "better," or the "best," and that took a long time. If the privy also had a Montgomery Ward catalogue, and ours did, it could take an eternity! Sometimes my behind would get numb from just looking at the pictures and I'd end up with a red halo around my rear-end from sitting on the hole for so long, but the pleasure was worth the pain!

Well, one day, after I finished eating a big breakfast at Grandma Wright's kitchen table, I headed out the back door and down the steps. I didn't get very far before Grandma called and asked me where I was going. I told her "I had to go see a man about a horse." Grandma just nodded her head and smiled (Grandma always understood). After all, little boys need a little "genuine relief" just like everybody else!

Just Plain Stuck

Have you ever been stuck – in a fix, a predicament – caught in a situation that no matter how hard you tried you just couldn't get out?

As I said earlier, kids need a little "genuine relief" just like grownups. But the need for "genuine relief" is a funny kind of thing – you never know just when it's going to make itself known. If you discover you need a little "genuine relief" during the day time, you head for the privy. But what if you need a little "genuine relief" in the middle of the night, then what do you do?

Papa had an answer for most everything, including what you do if you need a little "genuine relief" in the middle of the night. Papa put a pot that he called a "thunder bucket" beside everybody's bed so that if you needed a little "genuine relief" at night, you simply got out of bed and sat on the pot!

That's what I want to tell you about – what happened late one night when I tried to sit on the pot!

It was well past midnight when I woke up and the first thing I said to myself was, "I think I need a little "genuine relief." So I got out of bed and headed for the pot, but when I went to sit on it, my hand slipped and all of me except my arms, head and the lower part of my legs sank into the pot. I mean to tell you, I was stuck and no matter how hard I tried, I just couldn't get out.

The first to arrive on the scene were the dogs, Sam, Peggy and Dixie. Papa's dogs were a pretty smart bunch, and even though my rear-end was stuck in the pot, I could tell that they were having a little discussion amongst themselves – Peggy probably said, "It's always more exciting when John Walter is around" and Sam, being the oldest, probably said, "I think we have a real 'dis-ass-ter' on our hands."

Then, Grandma arrived holding an oil lamp. The lamp threw a good bit of light on my predicament, but it didn't do much toward freeing my rear-end. Finally, Papa and Uncle Seals arrived, but they didn't seem to take my predicament nearly as seriously as I was taking it. At first, they just stood there staring at me in a strange kinda way. Then Papa looked at Seals and said, "I don't recollect ever seeing anything quite like this, what do you reckon it is?" Uncle Seals said, "I think it's some kind of turtle that's flipped over on its back." Then Papa said, "No, it looks more like something hatching out of an egg to me."

By this time, Grandma, getting a little impatient with Papa and Uncle Seals' lack of seriousness said, "We need to do something to get this child out. We can't send him home with his rear end stuck in a pot." So, Uncle Seals picked up the pot with me in it while Papa grabbed my arms and legs and both began pulling in opposite directions. After a brief struggle, followed by a swoosh and a pop, my rear-end came sliding out of the pot.

The next day, Grandma took me aside and reminded me that there are lessons to be learned form each of life's experiences – and you know, Grandma was right – what I learned was that "genuine relief" can have more than one meaning . . . it can also mean having your butt pulled out of a pot in the middle of the night!

"Puttin' Me On"

My Uncle Seals took me with him just about everywhere he went. So, one day when he asked if I wanted to go bird hunting with him I naturally said, "yes." It wasn't long before we were headed down to the Old Moorhead place a few miles south of Buckhead where there were some open fields and hedgerows. Uncle Seals and Mr. Moorhead were good friends.

We took Sam and Dixie, the bird dogs, but left Peggy, the Boston bull terrier, home. Seals said, "Peggy doesn't know a bird from a beetle, and besides, her legs are too short; she can't keep up with the other dogs." Seals said that "even though Sam was too old to do much hunting, he still likes to go along, 'cause it makes him remember the good old days when he was younger. But Dixie, being young, can cover lots of ground and is good at locating and pointing birds."

As we moved across the field, Seals told me a lot of things about bird dogs and hunting and things like that. Then, all of a sudden he said, "Hold still, John Walter, and look way over there on the far side of the field." Sure enough, there was Dixie, frozen in space, standing perfectly still, not moving a muscle. "Dixie's pointing," whispered Uncle Seals. "Let's just move over there and then I'll signal her to flush the birds." So, that's what we did, me and Uncle Seals with his double-barrel shotgun eased up real close-like, about as close to Dixie as we could get without scaring the birds.

Then, Uncle Seals said, "John Walter, look where Dixie is pointing." "I'm looking," I said, and I was. Then, Seals looked over his shoulder and said, "John Walter, you're looking in the wrong direction." "No I'm not," I replied, "his tail is pointing this way!" Exasperated, Uncle Seals explained, "Bird dogs don't point with their tail, they point with their nose." I replied, "You didn't tell me which end of the dog to pay attention to, so, I just naturally looked in the direction his tail was pointing." By the time Uncle Seals had clarified which end of a bird dog is the end that does the pointing, the birds had flown away.

As we were heading back across the field, Seals told me about an old bird dog he used to have for duck hunting. Seals said, "That old dog could walk on water! Every time I shot a duck and it fell in the lake, that dog would just walk out across the water and fetch the duck." Seals said, "It was the 'darndest' thing" he'd ever seen! Then Seals just shook his head and said, "I never was able to teach that dog how to swim."

Now, I've heard some pretty strange things in my time, but I've never heard of a dog that could walk on water. So, the next day I asked Grandma about Uncle Seals' dog, the one that could walk on water. Grandma just smiled and said, "I think your Uncle Seals was just putting you on." Well, I'm a lot older now, and I want to tell you, I'm yet to see a dog that can walk on water. You know something, I think Uncle Seals was just 'putting me on'!

Seeing, Hearing and Remembering

Having eyes, do you not see,
and having ears, do you not hear?
And do you not remember?

Mark 8:18, RSV

Our human blindness is proverbial. We see a little and we miss much. However, if we are fortunate, in time, perhaps after many years, we will begin to see, hear and remember the love that sustained us all along.

It was Sunday, the day before I was to return home. Knowing that she would not see me again until the following summer, and how much I enjoyed her cooking, Grandma Wright prepared a special going away dinner for me. Spread before us were fried catfish that Papa, Uncle Seals and I had caught on trotlines down at the fish camp on the Apalachee River, all kinds of fresh vegetables from the garden, even quail and dove from Uncle Seals' last bird hunt. Uncle Seals reminded me to be careful 'cause sometimes there were a few birdshot left in the birds. There was a steaming pot of chicken and dumplings. Grandma always left enough of the chicken parts sticking up through the crust so that everyone would be able to find their favorite piece of chicken. Goldilocks, Papa's Jersey cow, provided the milk. Papa said, because we didn't have refrigeration, the only way to keep milk fresh was to keep it inside the cow until it was needed. Most of the time Goldie's milk was sweet tasting, but sometimes she would graze in a section of the pasture where there was bitter weed and her milk would have a bitter taste, but today it was good and sweet. Finally, Grandma had prepared my favorite – deep-pan blackberry pie with lots of sugar and fresh butter.

Usually Papa returned thanks, but Grandma said that she wanted to return thanks, so, we all bowed our heads. Grandma began by saying how much they had enjoyed my visit and asked God to see me safely through the winter so that we could be together again next summer. Then she thanked God for all that had been provided – the catfish that Papa, Seals and John Walter had caught, for the abundance of the years vegetable garden and especially for the blackberries that Papa and John Walter had picked on Saturday. (On Saturday, Grandma had supplied Papa and me with two tin pails and sent us about a mile down the dirt road toward Swords to a hedgerow where there were lots of blackberries). Grandma thanked God for everyone's good health and asked that the food be blessed to the nourishment of our bodies, that we might be enabled to care for the land, each other and the needs of others. Then Grandma paused, as though she had something further she wanted to say, but hadn't quite formed in her mind what it was. After a few moments she concluded her prayer . . . "And keep John Walter ever mindful that he will always be in our thoughts and prayers" . . . I think Grandma was trying to tell me something.

SWORDS

During most of the eighteenth century the Creek Indians remained dominant west of the Apalachee and Oconee Rivers. By the early nineteenth century, there were increasing signs of prosperity along these rivers in the area later known as Swords. Mills and other forms of commerce had sprung up. A riverboat plowed the waters of the Oconee as far south as Darien, Georgia. Around 1860, the area came to be called Blue Springs. It wasn't until the town of Swords was incorporated in 1906 that it officially became known as Swords.

Born in Carroll County, Georgia in 1859, John Buchanon Swords had experienced difficult times early in life. In 1864, his father was killed in the Confederate defense of Atlanta, leaving his mother with three young children to care for. Early on, Swords hired himself out to a gentleman in Carroll County for $8.00 per month for ten months and attended school the remaining two months. At the end of the year he had saved $53.00 of his $80.00 salary – early lessons learned during difficult times. Swords first came to Madison, Georgia in 1888 where he was in the distillery business. Around 1895, he began buying land in the Blue Springs area for $4.00 to $5.00 per acre. In time, he and his family would acquire a farm consisting of some three thousand acres.

During the first decade of the twentieth century, Swords literally built himself a town. An early attraction was the clear water provided by Blue Springs located behind his home, a much-needed resource for his distillery operation. Later, he built a large brick building to house the Swords Supply Company, the J.B. Swords Bank and the Swords Post Office. Across the street he constructed a two-story warehouse. Swords also operated a gristmill and a cotton gin, the first in Morgan County powered by a diesel engine. The gin processed over 1,600 bales of cotton annually, half of which was produced by Swords himself.

In 1910, Swords persuaded the Georgia Railroad to construct the Swords depot along with a six-car siding, thereby providing him with a facility for shipping timber and cotton along with liquor produced at his distillery. In 1912, he was instrumental in having the Swords Methodist Church built, a lovely country Gothic building. When his grandchildren came of school age, he constructed a two-room schoolhouse. The community also had two blacksmith shops, a jail and numerous houses for tenant farmers.

Early in the century, L.B. Chambers, who owned a large farm on the Greene County side of the Apalachee River adjacent to Sword's farm on the west bank in Morgan County, joined Swords to build the first bridge across the river at their own expense. Swords' motivation was to have the national highway between Madison and Greensboro come through Swords and Buckhead, thereby following the railroad and telephone lines and in so doing, enhance the value of his own holdings.

The intervening years between 1895 and 1921 were prosperous years for John "Buck" Swords and his family. By 1916, he had been elected to the Georgia State House of Representatives and in 1919 as a Morgan County Commissioner. It has been estimated that throughout most of the first two decades of the twentieth century, his gross income from his various enterprises was well in excess of $200,000 annually.

The eventual demise of the town of Swords can be attributed to a number of causes. Perhaps, John "Buck" Swords' unsuccessful attempt to have the national highway routed through Swords and Buckhead can, in retrospect, be viewed as a bad omen. The 1919 ratification of the Eighteenth Amendment to the Constitution prohibiting the "manufacture, sale or transportation of any intoxicating liquors" ended his lucrative distillery business. The 1921 arrival of an almost invisible grayish critter known as the boll weevil destroyed two-thirds of the cotton crop, thereby striking a lethal blow to the local economy. As if the boll weevil had not wrought enough destruction, in August of 1924, the Swords cotton gin was struck by lightning and burned to the ground at a loss of $25,000. Notwithstanding these and other adversities, Swords, surrounded by family, continued to live a comfortable life in the community he had built until his death in 1940.

"Great-granddaddy Swords"
John Buchanon Swords
1859-1940

"Su Briney"
Su Briney Moon Swords
1861-1923

John "Buck" Swords was born in Carroll County, Georgia. In 1864 his father was killed during the Confederate defense of Atlanta. In 1880 he married Su Briney Moon from Logansville, Georgia. Upon moving to Morgan County, Georgia, they lived briefly in Rutledge before moving to Madison in 1888. A Madisonian article dated May 8, 1914 by C.M. Furlow, described John "Buck" Swords as "A captain of Industry, and pioneer Builder and Developer." In addition to business interests in Madison, he began acquiring land in the Blue Springs area of the county in 1895 and over time, acquired a farm consisting of some three thousand acres of land. Beyond building and incorporating the town of Swords, of which he was mayor, he owned the J.B. Swords Supply Company, the Swords Distillery, and was President of the J.B. Swords Bank. In 1914, his cotton gin, the first in Morgan County operated by a diesel engine, turned out over 1600 bales of cotton, half of which he had produced. In 1916 he was elected to the Georgia State House of Representatives and in 1919 he was elected County Commissioner of the Shepard's, Buckhead, Kingston and Martins Districts of Morgan County. John "Buck Swords and Su Briney Swords had three children: Leonidas Cramer (1881-1958), Lula May (1883-1935) and Jessie Leater (1894-1981), who is shown in the photograph with her parents. The Swords are buried in the Swords' Community Cemetery with other family members. The photograph was taken in Madison, circa 1899.

The Former Home of John Buchanon and Su Briney Moon Swords

"*Granddaddy Bond*" "*Lula May*"
Emory Allen Bond ***Lula May Swords Bond***

1877-1944 ***1883-1935***

*E*mory Allen Bond was born in Franklin County, Georgia. He lived most of his adult life in the community of Swords in Morgan County, Georgia where he was closely associated with his father-in-law, John "Buck" Swords. Emory owned and operated a gristmill in addition to extensive farming and timber interests in the Swords area. He was a member of the Board of Directors of the Farmer's Fire Insurance Company in Madison, Georgia. He was also an active member of the Buckhead Masonic Lodge. Emory and Lula May were married in 1903 and had two children: the author's mother, Mildred Elizabeth (1906-

1979) and Clinton Emory (1909-1973). Lula May attended Georgia College for Women in Milledgeville, Georgia. Until her death in 1935 she served as postmistress for the Swords community. Emory and Lula May were charter members of the Swords Methodist Church where for many years Lula May taught the young people's Sunday school class. Emory and Lula May are buried with other family members in the Swords Community Cemetery. The photograph was taken circa 1911.

*The Former Home of Emory Allen and
Lula May Swords Bond*

The Bonds built the house in 1919-20.

SWORDS

"Uncle John Hill"
John Hill Cochran

1887-1984

"Aunt Jessie"
Jessie Leater Swords Cochran

1894-1981

John Hill Cochran was born in the southern part of Morgan County, Georgia, where his foreparents first settled in the early 1800's prior to the county's formulation in 1807. In 1912 he married Jessie Leater Swords. John Hill was a veteran of the First World War, having served as a sergeant in the medical corps in France. Later, he owned and operated the Swords General Store, along with other interests related to farming, livestock and timber. In these and other interests, he was closely associated with his father-in-law, John "Buck" Swords. He was honored by the Morgan County Board of Commissioners for his thirty-five years of public service as commissioner from the Swords area and nineteen years as Chairman of the County Board of Tax Appraisers. Jessie was born in Madison, Georgia, the daughter of John Buchanon and Su Briney Swords. She attended Cox College in Atlanta. John Hill and Jessie lived in Swords most of their lives where they were charter members of the Swords Methodist Church and active in community affairs. In 1947, on the occasion of John Hill's retirement, they moved to Madison where they lived the remainder of their lives. They had no children and are buried in the Swords Community Cemetery The photographs were taken circa 1910.

The Former Home of John Hill and Jessie Swords Cochran

The house was built by the Cochrans in 1914.

The Home of
Leonidas Cramer and Alma Louise King Swords

The house was built in 1919 and destroyed by fire in the early 1990's.

The Swords United Methodist Church

A country Gothic church built in 1912.

The Swords General Store known earlier as The J.B. Swords Supply Company

Constructed circa 1900, the building also housed the J.B. Swords Bank and the Swords Post Office. The store was first operated by John "Buck" Swords and later by his son-in-law, John Hill Cochran. The store was destroyed by fire circa 1990.

John "Buck" Swords built this house around 1910.

Swords built the house for the purpose of having a place to drink and play cards with his friends and business associates. The house was destroyed by fire circa 2000.

The Swords Depot

In 1910 John "Buck" Swords, persuaded the Georgia Railroad to construct the Swords Depot along with a six car siding, thereby providing him with a facility for shipping timber, cotton and liquor produced at his distillery. The photograph was taken in 1953 by W.F. Bechum, Jr. prior to the depot's removal in 1956.

The Swords Jailhouse

Built in the early 20th century. Destroyed by fire in the late 1990's.

The Old Swords Bridge

Built circa 1913, the bridge spanned the Apalachee River separating Morgan and Greene Counties. In 1978 the bridge fell victim to the rising waters of lake Oconee, and was removed. The photo first appeared in the June 9, 1977 edition of The Madisonian.

The Day We Buried Lula May

Her married name was Lula May Swords Bond. She was born June 21, 1883. Lula May died Monday, April 22, 1935 at four o'clock in the afternoon at the McGeary Hospital in Madison. Her friends knew her affectionately as "Miss Lula May." I called her Grandma, 'cause she was Grandma to me.

> Death lies on her like
> an untimely frost upon
> the fairest flower of all
> the field.
>
> *– Shakespeare*

I was only three years old when my Grandma Bond died, but I remember some things about the day we buried her – my Mom told me some other things and over the years some of the older folks have added to what I remember. I remember how quiet everyone was up at the big house that morning. As Mom dressed me, making sure my clothes were just right, how she would say in a soft voice, "Now, we want to look nice for Grandma."

Soon, we were all in the car headed to the church. Dad drove with Granddaddy Bond sitting up front beside him; Mom and I sat on the back seat. I remember how sad everyone was. Most of all, I wasn't sure just how to act or feel. It was my first funeral and I wasn't sure what it meant. Would I ever see Grandma again? Would she be able to read stories to me again? Where will Grandma go and what will happen to her?

When we arrived at the Swords Methodist Church, I realized that it must be a pretty special day. Cars were parked all over the church yard and down both sides of the dirt road – further than I had ever seen before. The church was so full of people that many had to stand even after they brought in extra chairs.

We took our place beside my Great-granddaddy Swords, Lula May's father, and next to my Great-aunt Jessie and Uncle John Hill Cochran – Aunt Jessie was Lula May's younger sister. Just in front of us was Lula May's open casket. As the service began a quartet composed of Mrs. Purks[1], Mrs. Ray[2], Mr. Atkinson[3], and Mr. Furlow[4], accompanied by Mrs. Vason[5] at the piano, sang "Peace be Still" and "Take Time to be Holy."

Then, Reverend Chapple[6], the pastor of the church, read from the Gospel of John, Chapter 14:1-17 – Lula May's favorite scripture:

> Let not your heart be troubled:
> Ye believe in God, believe also in
> me. In my Father's house are many
> mansions: if it were not so, I would
> have told you. And if I go and prepare
> a place for you I will come again, and
> receive you unto myself; that where I
> am, there ye may be also …

I didn't altogether understand the scripture, but it sounded pretty reassuring – at least Grandma would have a nice place to stay!

The scripture reading was followed by some kind words from Lula May's favorite former pastor, Reverend Hoke Sewell[7]. Rev. Sewell began by saying that "in the death of Lula May, Morgan County had lost one of its most beloved women citizens." He spoke of how "she taught a large Sunday school class," how she had "instructed the young folks most beautifully every Sabbath and then lived her religion all during the week, day in and day out, month by month, year by year."

Rev. Sewell further recalled how she had "stood by her pastor, her church and her Lord at all times." He spoke of how she had been "an integral factor in the social, civic and religious life of the little community of Swords, which she loved so much." He recalled how "her father, the Honorable John "Buck" Swords, the founder and builder of the village which bears his name, had erected the very church in which we were sitting and the nearby parsonage." As Rev. Sewell told of the many "beautiful deeds" performed by this "modern Dorcas," there were many eyes wet with tears and many hearts filled by emotions of poignant grief. Gazing down at Lula May's hands, silently folded across her bosom, Rev. Sewell proclaimed that "they had been twin sisters of mercy and that her feet had been swift to run on errands of love, goodwill and hope." In a prayerful attitude, Rev. Sewell concluded: "And now may the fragrance of her unselfish life abide through the years to cheer and bless the lives of others, and may the blessings of God be continued to the bereaved."

To tell the truth, I had never thought of Grandma as a "modern Dorcas." To be honest, I didn't know what an "old Dorcas" was, much less a "modern Dorcas." Anyway, I knew that Lula May and Rev. Sewell were old friends, so whatever he said must have been good if it was about Grandma. Later I learned that Dorcus meant a Christian woman of New Testament times who made clothing for the poor.

Following Rev. Sewell's eulogy, Mr. Hemperley[8], the local undertaker, rose from his pew, and with his deep baritone voice slowly and with great authority, began singing:

> On a hill far away stood
> an old rugged Cross, the
> emblem of suffering and
> shame...

Well, I must say, Mr. Hemperley's rendering of "The Old Rugged Cross" left an everlasting impression on one little boy that day, 'cause to this day, I can still see that old rugged cross on that hill far away!

As we neared the end of the service, a line formed and everyone slowly passed by Lula May's casket to pay their last respects – the white folks came first, followed by the black folks who had been standing in the rear of the church. After that, we all followed the hearse carrying Lula May's body to the Swords Cemetery atop a nearby hill, where on that April day in '35, my Mother held my hand as we made our way to its crest[9]. Soon, all were gathered around the gravesite, the black folks on the outer edge of the circle – and then, as

Rev. Sewell was concluding the graveside service with the words:

> For as much as the spirit of
> the departed hath returned to
> God who gave it, we therefore
> commit Lula May's body to
> the ground, earth to earth,
> ashes to ashes, dust to dust...

As he spoke these words while tossing a handful of earth upon her casket, someone began to sing softly:

> Farther along we'll know all about it,
> Farther along we'll understand why,
> Cheer up my brother, live in the sunshine,
> We'll understand it all by and by...

and soon everyone had joined in as Lula May's body was gently entrusted to earth's embrace. For many years my mother returned to memories' sacred soil, and there, caressed by summer's warmth, would carefully groom the grave and plant fresh flowers – for many years I've also returned.

Notes

1. Mrs. J.H. Purks was a very petite lady whose husband was a school principal in Madison. They were both well thought of in the Madison community.

2. Mrs. Taylor (Mildred Snellings) Ray was a postal employee in the Madison post office. She loved the color purple and wore it often. She also loved flowers and kept a vase of flowers sitting in the postal window – always a conversation piece.

3. Mr. Everett G. Atkinson was cashier at the Bank of Madison most of his adult life and was known as an honest man who cared for others.

4. Mr. Charles M. Furlow, a close friend of John 'Buck' Swords and his family since 1894 when Mr. Furlow was appointed Postmaster by President Grover Cleveland. Mr. Furlow said, "The bond required was a large one. The only man in all Morgan County who voluntarily signed my bond was John B. Swords." Early in the century he had served as Clerk of the Morgan County Superior Court, and from 1925 until 1929, Mayor of Madison. He did not like to drive so his wife always drove him in their little Chevrolet.

5. Mrs. Joseph (Madeline) Vason was the wife of Joe Vason of the Vason Brothers Drug Store in Madison, later known as the Madison Drug Company. Madeline was a talented musician, a civic leader in Morgan County and campaigned for many projects that helped to make Madison what it is today.

6. Rev. W.E Chapple was pastor of the Swords Methodist Church in 1935 at the time of Lula May's death.

7   Rev. Hoke Sewell first became known to our family when, in the early 1930's he served the Swords Methodist Church while a seminary student at Emory University in Atlanta. Hoke went on to become a prominent Methodist minister in the North Georgia Annual Conference of the Methodist Church. He remained a close personal friend of the family and at their request officiated at a number of subsequent family funerals.

8   Mr. Walter C. Hemperley owned and operated Hemperley Funeral Home from 1911 until 1968. He owned and flew his own airplane and promoted aviation in Morgan County. He worked tirelessly for defense programs and was active in Red Cross and disaster relief programs of the Second World War. Mr. Hemperley had a beautiful baritone voice and a reputation for conducting funeral services with his eyes, never having to make a gesture with his hands.

9   The pall-bearers were: Carroll Hunt, Everette Hill, Herman Mitchem, William Yearwood, Frank Cox, Jack Hobbs, Herbert Millwood and Vesta Mitchem.

All were friends of Lula May. Internment was in the Swords Cemetery.

Downright Mortified

The day got off to a pretty slow start. I left the big house up at Granddaddy Bond's and made my usual rounds. First, I swung down by Uncle John Hill's store and checked things out down there and then I swung by the gristmill – I liked to smell the freshly ground corn and run my hands through it. Then I made my way to the blacksmith shop. It was always exciting to work the bellows and see the coals turn red hot! Finally, I headed up to Granddaddy Bond's pasture, opened the gate and had a little talk with the horses and cows. By now, it was time to head back to Granddaddy's place for lunch.

As I said, the day got off to a pretty slow start, but it didn't stay that way very long. About the time I finished lunch, I heard Uncle John Hill shouting, "Willie, get up to the church and head 'um off up there!" Then I heard Fred Sanders shouting to somebody to "get those mules off the railroad tracks before the midday train comes!" The whole town was in an uproar. Granddaddy Bond was hollering to Vince, one of the wage hands, to "clear those horses out of the backyard before they trample the flower beds and get in the garden!" When I stuck my head out the front door to see what was going on, I couldn't believe my eyes. There were more farm animals roaming around Swords than people – in fact, a lot more!

In one direction, there was a bunch of cows heading up the dirt road toward Buckhead (they'd probably never been to Buckhead and just wanted to see what the place looked like). Then there were five or six horses standing around the depot as if they were waiting for the next train. And down at the blacksmith's shop there were two mules standing face to face as if they were having a discussion – probably a couple of Democrats discussing F.D.R's upcoming election! Animals all over the place – you would have thought Noah's Ark landed in the middle of Swords and Noah forgot and left the door open!

Well, naturally I wanted to help, so I ran down the road to where Uncle John Hill and Granddaddy Bond were standing and asked if I could help. They looked at me in a strange kinda way and said, "You've already supplied just about all the help we can handle for one day!" And then they did something that affected me the rest of my life. Each grabbed an arm and led me off down the road. As we passed Aunt Jessie's house, she asked Uncle John Hill, "What are ya'all going to do to that child?" A little further on, we passed Great-granddaddy Swords' house where he was sitting on the front porch. As we passed by, he called out, "Throw the little bugger in jail!" And that's just what they did, they threw me in jail!

I'd been sent to my room a few times in my life, but being thrown in the Swords jail and having to view the world from behind bars was something else. Can you imagine being imprisoned by your own family and having to do time at the tender age of seven? Why, I was downright mortified!! Well, after about two hours Aunt Jessie managed to bail me out on the condition that in the future I would always remember to shut the pasture gate following my daily visit with the horses and cows.

Two hours of jail time is a lot of time, and it affected me the rest of my life. To this day, if I see something that's open, I shut it – I shut everything in sight – refrigerator doors, car doors, house doors, cabinet doors, drawers, windows... You name it and I'll shut it!

Growing Up

I suppose growing up wouldn't be so hard if you just had more experience at doing it! If only you had grown up two or three times before, you'd kinda know what to expect but this being the first time you've ever done it, you just don't have much experience to go on, and that was pretty much what I was up against – no experience!

As I remember, I was seven years old, so, it must have been during the summer of 1939. I was down at Granddaddy Bond's house in Swords when my baby teeth began to come unhinged. It always puzzled me why the Lord would give you teeth that have to come out in the first place. After all, just because you're growing up, your arms and legs don't come loose and have to be replaced! Why teeth?

I told Granddaddy Bond about my problem and he made it all sound real simple – "just tie a string around your tooth and then tie the string to a door knob, then shut your eyes and slam the door and your tooth will come right out . . . just like that!" It sounded pretty simple to me. So, I did what he said; I tied one end of the string around my tooth and the other end around a door knob – then I shut my eyes, and as I was about to slam the door, what had seemed pretty simple, all of a sudden got complicated. What Granddaddy

Bond told me seemed simple enough, but he must have left something out. I tried several different doors, but it didn't help – nothing changed – each time I closed my eyes and was about to slam the door, what seemed simple, all of a sudden got real complicated.

There's nothing like a little pain to help focus your mind, and it was the painful part that Granddaddy Bond forgot to tell me about. You see, it's simple enough to jump out a window or bang your head against a stonewall, but it's also painful and it was the painful part that Granddaddy Bond forgot to mention. So, every time I shut my eyes and was about to slam the door, it was the painful part that made it all so complicated. Now that the painful part had focused my mind, I had to figure out a more pleasant way to get my teeth to come out – besides, Granddaddy Bond said the tooth fairy would probably give me about ten cents a tooth, which helped focus my mind even more!

It was about this time that I remembered something that me and my friend, Junebug, had been up to. . . something that gave me an idea as to a more pleasant way to get my teeth to come out. Unbeknownst to Granddaddy Bond, me and Junebug had been feeding one of his bird dogs some sticky peanut butter. It was so funny to watch that dog trying to eat that sticky peanut butter that you just had to laugh! The dog really liked the peanut butter but every time he got a mouthful and tried to chew, he couldn't hardly get his mouth open! Now, my thinking was, that if the dog's teeth had been loose, the sticky peanut butter woulda helped pull 'em out at the same time he was enjoying the peanut butter!

So, with that in mind, me and Junebug took off down to Uncle John Hill's general store where we knew we could get some hard chewy caramel candy, and sure enough, it worked. I started chewing and by the end of the day I had more teeth in my pocket than I knew what to do with – and furthermore, it was a pretty enjoyable experience!

Best of all, the tooth fairy did give me ten cents for each tooth and in 1939, ten cents went a long way – for ten cents, me and Junebug could buy two Three-Center soft drinks and four big one cent sugar cookies – growing up wasn't so bad after all!

Take It to the Cows in Prayer

Each summer when I'd visit my Granddaddy Bond in Swords, the first thing I would do was make out for the pigpen and give all the pigs a name – not just any kind of name but highfalutin' names like Jeffery, Magnolia, Elizabeth and Reginald.

A lot of times grown-ups are in too big a hurry or just plain don't understand what's bothering you, but you still need a friend and somebody to talk to. On the other hand, pigs are never in a hurry and they are always looking for a friend. In fact, pigs can be pretty understanding. The pigs and I had a few other things in common – we all liked to eat and none of us had much use for soap! Ole Reginald was my favorite pig, cause he was a good listener. Reginald would come over and let me scratch his side while I talked to him, and from time to time he would let out with a grunt, as if to say, "You are absolutely right, sometimes grown-ups just don't understand."

Well, everything was going along pretty good, at least I thought it was, until my visit the following summer. Naturally, the first thing I did was to head down to the pigpen, but Reginald was nowhere to be found. In fact, there was a completely new bunch of pigs. I asked Granddaddy what had happened to Reginald and he said, "Reginald had undergone a kind of conversion." "Was it a religious conversion?" I asked. "No," he said, "last fall Reginald was converted into sausage."

Well, it took a while for the full impact, that is to say, the deeper implication of Reginald's conversion to sink in. It was about that time that I shifted my affections from Granddaddy Bond's pigpen to the barnyard where the cows were. I know the old hymn says to "Take it to the Lord in prayer," but I found it easier to talk to the cows. In fact, I not only talked to the cows, I began the high and honorable practice of "cow confessing."

Actually, cows work better than pigs. A cow will listen to just about anything, and confessing to a cow is a lot less painful than confessing to Mom and Dad, preachers or even the Lord. The way it works is, you get face-to-face with the cow – most any cow will do – and then you confess to the cow's front end. The cow then processes your confession and expels it in the form of gas – a kind of recycling process! The beauty of this form of confession is that it provides relief to both you and the cow! Best of all, cows are forgiving, they don't get upset with you – they'll be right there tomorrow, waiting to hear more confessions as if nothing ever happened!

P.S. Make sure you use a cow and not a bull – confessing to a bull can be deadly and lead to meeting your maker sooner than desired!

"I'll Fly Away"

I think it was the summer of 1939. I was staying at my Granddaddy Bond's house in Swords. His first name was Emory. Most everyone called him "Em" except me; I called him Granddaddy. Grandma's name was Lula May – Lula May was my Greatgranddaddy Swords' daughter. She died in 1935 when I was three years old. I remember sitting on her lap once while she read to me from a storybook and the day we buried her.

Lord, it was hot. The windows were open and the breeze caused the curtains to flutter as high as the top of my head. Off in another section of the house, Granddaddy Bond's radio was playing gospel music. The Jordanaires were singing, "I'll Fly Away," and fly away I did! I took off down the dirt road, past the gristmill and on past Uncle John Hill's general store to get my friend, Junebug. Junebug was Essiebell's little boy – Essiebell lived in a house behind my Aunt Jessie and Uncle John Hill's house and was their cook. Well, I found Junebug and we headed toward the Apalachee River for a cool swim. I wasn't wearing anything but a pair of shorts, no shirt or shoes. All Junebug had on was a pair of bib overalls. We made our way across the creek, past the Swords Methodist Church and on past the cemetery located atop the hill on the left hand side of the road.

As you know, life is never simple – there's always a little pain before you get to the good part. At least that's what Granddaddy Bond always said and I think he was right. Sure enough, I experienced plenty of pain before we reached the river. It was early summer and the bottom of my feet had not had time to toughen up. The road that lay between us and the cool waters of the Apalachee River was hot and rocky, like walking across a bed of hot coals in order to get to the cookie jar. Lord, it was hot! We could see the bridge that crossed the river from Morgan to Greene County but it was like walking through the valley of the shadow of death to get there. After much hop, skipping and jumping, we made it, crossed the bridge, made a left turn and headed up the bank to our favorite swimming hole. It wasn't long before my shorts and Junebug's bib overalls were hanging from a tree limb and we were buck-naked! We had our swim, but decided we didn't need any more pain, so we enjoyed each other's company until early evening when the road had cooled down before heading home.

Lord, Have Mercy On My Soul

I remember, it was late autumn, 1937. I was five years old. I suppose the reason I remember is because my brother Allen was born in February of 1938—but I'll get back to that later.

My mother and I were staying at my Granddaddy Bond's house in Swords – the big house with the tall columns and porch that extended around three sides of the house. But for a number of reasons, I liked to hang out about half-a-mile down a dirt road at my Uncle John Hill and Aunt Jessie's house. One reason was that Aunt Jessie and her cook, Essiebell, always kept a good supply of food on hand. But there was another, even more special reason. You see, my Uncle John Hill was a soldier in France during the First World War and when he returned home in 1919, he brought all his Army stuff home and hung it on some pegs in his barn. There was a gas mask, a pair of leggings, a Red Cross medical bag and some other things. It was always exciting to wear Uncle John Hill's Army things and pretend to be a soldier, but sometimes it got me into a lot of trouble. One day I put on Uncle John Hill's gas mask and proceeded to walk down a long hallway into Aunt Jessie's kitchen where she was busy cooking. When she turned around and saw me, she let out a blood-curdling scream. I scared her half to death! Later, she told my mother that I looked like a two legged, shrunk up baby elephant.

My favorite thing among Uncle John Hill's Army stuff was his steel army helmet, which also got me in trouble with Aunt Jessie. On this particular day my mother had to go to a nearby town, so she left me in the care of Aunt Jessie. I was wearing Uncle John Hill's helmet and playing "Army" with my friend, Billy Moon. Billy asked me why soldiers wore steel helmets. Being an expert in these matters, I told him, "they wore steel helmets so enemy bullets wouldn't go through their heads." Billy found this hard to believe, so we set out to see if it really was true. Billy got his BB gun and I bent over with Uncle John Hill's helmet on my head. Things were going pretty good – Billy firing away at my head and the bullets pinging off the helmet in all directions – I say things were going pretty good until Aunt Jessie, who was supposed to be taking care of me, appeared at the front door and shouted, "Lord, have mercy on my soul, why on earth anyone would want to have children I do not know!"

Well, the experience of my head being used for target practice in her own front yard was more than she could handle. As they used to say, "it was the last straw, the one that finally broke the camel's back." Uncle John Hill agreed that if he and Aunt Jessie were going to survive my visits they would have to hide Uncle John Hill's Army stuff, which they did!

But, just because they hid the stuff didn't mean that I couldn't try to find it and that's just what I set out to do. I looked all over the place, in the barn, under the house, all over the place. Most of all, I wanted to find the helmet, and then, for the first time, I noticed how big my mother's stomach was! Could it be? I could hardly believe my eyes – she had hidden the helmet under her dress! So, I asked, "Why is your stomach so big?" Her response was, "It's none of your business." Then, I accused her of hiding the helmet under her dress and she responded, "There is no helmet under my dress!" Then I asked if I could look – and you know what, to this day I don't know why she wouldn't let me look. Well, I never did find the helmet, but in February I had a new baby brother!

Between a Rock and a Hard Place

My Aunt Jessie was a very opinionated woman as anyone who knew her would tell you, and one of Aunt Jessie's many opinions was that when you were called to dinner, you were supposed to stop whatever you were doing and come ... NOW! So, when Aunt Jessie shouted out the kitchen window, "John Walter, come to dinner!" it was like hearing the voice of God and as most people know, God doesn't like having to call twice and neither did Aunt Jessie!

As I recall, I was around six years old, which means that what I'm going to tell you about took place during the summer of 1938 down at Aunt Jessie's house in Swords. You see, there was this little creek – it ran behind Uncle John Hill's general store, under a bridge near the Swords Methodist Church and on behind the barn next to Aunt Jessie's house. As the creek ran past the barn, it passed over a large rock and on the other side of the rock, the creek became a big round pond – In fact, it was one of my favorite swimming holes; and it was within shouting distance of Aunt Jessie's kitchen window.

It was hot as Hades that day, so Junebug (Essiebell's little boy) and I decided to have a swim, and since no one could see us behind Uncle John Hill's barn, we decided to skinny-dip – which as everybody knows is by far the best way to go swimming, especially if you can get away with it! So, we took our clothes off and laid them up next to the barn.

Uncle John Hill saw what was going on and unbeknownst to me and Junebug, he decided he'd have a little fun at our expense! Uncle John Hill knew how impatient Aunt Jessie was, so he reckoned that if he could quietly snatch our clothes and hide them, then he'd just lay low and see what happened when Aunt Jessie called me to dinner. And that's just what he did. When we weren't looking, he snatched our clothes and hid them.

Sure enough, it wasn't long before Aunt Jessie stuck her head out the kitchen window and called, "John Walter, dinner is ready!" So, me and Junebug headed up to the barn to get our clothes, but they were nowhere to be found. Pretty soon, Aunt Jessie stuck her head out the kitchen window again and hollered, "John Walter, I don't want to have to call you again, dinner is ready!" Now, me and Junebug didn't know what to do – it was like being between a rock and a hard place. So, for a while, we just stood there looking at each other – and all the while Uncle John Hill was hiding in the barn with our clothes, laughing his head off!

The next time Aunt Jessie called, the earth shook. This time she shouted, "John Walter, this is the last time I intend to call. If you don't get yourself in here, I'm coming after you!" Well, when God calls, you move, that's all there is to it, it's just that simple. And move we did! Buck-naked, me and Junebug paraded past the barn to the back steps of Aunt Jessie's house where we stood face to face with God.

As Aunt Jessie peered down at us in utter exasperation, she came forth with her usual, "Lord have mercy on my soul!" – but this time she added, "Children!" – "forgive them, for they know not what they do!" Aunt Jessie liked to quote from the Bible.

Tramps, Hobos, and the Swords Depot

Historians of the Depression-era estimate that as many as four million people were involved in the romance of jumping freight trains in search of food, work or adventure. The hobo is defined as a man who travels to work; a tramp as a man who travels and won't work, and a bum as a man who just plain won't work; and a hobo jungle as an encampment where hobos gathered and a Hoover blanket as a newspaper. Hobos often were smooth talkers. Their ability to spin tall tales served as a form of "barter" as they rode the rails "westbound to heaven."

I want to tell you about the privilege of meeting Mr. Henry Ford's first cousin and a politician by the name of Wendell Wilkie up at the Swords depot.

I used to spend a lot of time hanging around the Swords Depot. For the most part I had the place pretty much to myself except at midday when uncle John Hill came up to "hang" the mailbag. In addition to owning the Swords General Store, Uncle John Hill was the Swords postmaster and the depot agent for the Georgia Railroad.

As I said, I usually had the place pretty much to myself, but one day I found a man with a long beard and a funny looking hat sleeping on one of the benches in the waiting room where the passengers waited for the train. When he woke up, we had a long conversation and, in the course of our conversation, he asked me if I knew who Mr. Henry Ford was. I said, no, I had never heard of Mr. Ford. Then, he told me that Mr. Henry Ford invented the Ford motorcar and that he was Henry Ford's first cousin. Sounded pretty impressive to me! As I was about to head back down to Uncle John Hill's store, the man asked me if I could lend him a nickel, that he would repay me the next time he came to Swords. So, I lent him my last nickel and headed on down to Uncle John Hill's store.

I told Uncle John Hill all about meeting Mr. Henry Ford's first cousin up at the depot. John Hill agreed that Henry Ford was a pretty important fellow and suggested that I might want to spend more time at the depot – that if I spent more time up there, I just might meet some of John D. Rockefeller and Cornelius Vanderbilt's kin folks. Sounded pretty exciting to me, so I did what Uncle John Hill suggested and began spending more time up at the depot.

As it turned out, I never did meet any of Mr. Rockefeller or Mr. Vanderbilt's family, but one day I did meet a fellow – said he had been a politician – that his name was Wendell Wilkie or something like that. When I was about to leave, he asked me if I could "spare a dime?" I told him I didn't have a dime, but that I could let him have a nickel. He said that would do fine and that he would repay me the next time he came through Swords. So, I headed on down to the Swords General Store to tell Uncle John Hill about my meeting with Mr. Wilkie, the politician. Uncle John Hill just scratched his head and mumbled something about "You shouldn't give your entire fortune to the rich and famous, save some for us poor folks."

You know something? The Swords Depot is a lot like Grand Central Station. If you hang around long enough, you will eventually meet some real interesting people.

The Swords General Store

My Uncle John Hill had himself a world. As we enter the twenty-first century, many of us find ourselves living at the outer edge of someone else's world. But Uncle John Hill had his own world and at its center was the Swords General store.

I can see him even now – short of stature, very serious and businesslike, wearing spectacles, a tie and long sleeve shirt with garters around each sleeve to keep them from interfering with his work. John Hill was also very methodical. As sure as the sun rose, at 7:30 each morning, John Hill, with his characteristic fast jerky gait, could be seen carrying a bucket of water in each hand, heading up the dirt road from his house to his red brick store. On reaching the store his first act of the day was to flip water from his buckets on to the floor in order to keep the dust down before sweeping the entire store.

Approaching the store, the first thing one saw were two Standard Oil gas pumps; one for regular gas and the other for premium. On one side of the pumps was a long handle and at the top was a round glass globe inside of which were numbers running from one through ten. Using the handle, you pumped into the glass globe the number of gallons you wanted and then let it run out by gravity. The next thing you saw before entering the store was a large red sign with white lettering affixed to the front of the building that read: "Drink Coca-Cola."

Upon entering one faced a red Coca-Cola soft drink chest behind which was a table containing all kinds of blue denim overalls and work clothes. To the right was the cash register along with three sections of glass cases supported by a long counter. The glass cases contained tobacco goods, candy and bread. Behind the glass cases was a wall filled with canned goods that reached all the way to the ceiling, in front of which was a moveable ladder that enabled John Hill to retrieve items that could not be reached from the floor. Looking to one's left was a wall containing all kinds of shoes, including work shoes, women's and children's shoes. Out from the wall were more glass cases in which jewelry and accessories were kept. Atop one of the cases was an old oak spool chest with drawers on each of its four sides filled with variously colored spools of thread. Beside the spool chest were two cases of pocketknives. Further along the wall were rolls of cloth: cheesecloth to cover table tops, cloth for making clothing, curtains and for other household uses. Beyond the rolls of cloth were racks of vegetable and flower seeds.

Extending across the back of the store was an oak partition with iron fencing along its top, behind which extended a long desk. This more 'official section' of the store housed the Swords Post Office and the J.B. Swords Bank, with its rather formidable walk-in vault. Facing the rear of the store, and about two-thirds of the way down the center aisle was a circle of chairs and a checkerboard table in the midst of which was a huge black pot-bellied stove – a kind of social circle, if you will. Behind the wall containing the canned goods was the other half of the store. There one found tables of salted side meat and hams, all covered with burlap bags to keep the flies away. There was a row of big wooden zinc-lined ice chests containing eggs, cheese, watermelons and cantaloupe. Against another wall were farm implements: thrashers, grinders, peelers along with plows, hoes, rakes, axes, even barrels of nails that were weighed and sold by the pound.

Beside the store were chicken coops and a pigpen for those who brought chickens and pigs for barter. Across the dirt road in front of the store stood a large, two-story wooden warehouse where John Hill kept less frequently called for items such as pumps, and pine caskets along with mule-drawn rakes and tillers. I cannot begin to recall all the items in that store. More than once I've heard people say, "John Hill had the best run and stocked general store in all of North Georgia."

Noontime was a particularly busy time. As late as 1940 it was not uncommon to see at least two horses along with two or three mule-drawn wagons tied to the posts supporting the corrugated tin roof extending from the front of the store. What occasioned the noontime rush was the arrival of the midday train and especially the incoming and outgoing mail. By the time I came along in the mid '30's, Lula May, John Hill's sister-in-law, had passed on, leaving the postmaster's job to John Hill. As soon as he "hung" the outgoing mail and retrieved the canvas bag containing the incoming mail, he would hurry back to the post office and begin calling out the names of those who had received mail. The women of the community, knowing the menfolk would be at the store to pick up the mail, would send lists of food items needed for lunch and dinner – thus, the noontime rush. I have a vivid recollection of Macon Moore and his son, Rich, at noon – carrying feed bags to put their goods in, having walked all the way from their farm on Parks Mill road, about two miles through the woods before reaching the railroad tracks which they would then follow down to the store – and old Ambrose Sanders who always arrived on his gray horse. After getting his mail and food, he would put them in two feedbags, tie the ends together, and drape them over his horse's neck and head home. Adding to the noontime congestion were wage hands taking their midday lunch break consisting of saltine crackers, sardines and a Coca-Cola. Noontime was a busy time!

As I said, my Uncle John Hill had himself a world and loved being flat-dab in the center of it. In present day terms, the Swords General Store was a Wal-Mart, a Sears & Roebuck, a Home Depot, a U.S. Post Office, a bank and a filling station, all rolled into one. Because John Hill was both the postmaster and the depot agent, all shipping of cotton and timber went through him. Since there was no local newspaper, few cars and virtually no telephones, the store also served as a kind of nerve center – a place where current news and gossip were conveyed. Beside the front door was a bulletin board on which messages might be posted. The store was also a place where local people came to barter. It was common for people to bring pigs, chickens, eggs, watermelons, and fresh vegetables in exchange for other things needed. John Hill's network of suppliers extended to Atlanta, Athens, Augusta, and beyond. As one old timer said, "You could find anything from cameo pins to caskets and everything in between at the Swords General Store."

An interesting characteristic of the store was its seasonal nature. John Hill had a kind of seasonal clock in his head. As spring and planting time approached, he made sure he had those things the farmers needed. Fall and winter brought forth their own needs. Families were consulted regarding toys and other gift items desired for Christmas. At Easter, women would make known their preferences regarding hats and new outfits for the children. Each of these considerations took on an individual quality and were addressed well ahead of time so that John Hill could consult with his suppliers about the availability of particular items.

As you might suspect by now, the Swords General Store and my Uncle John Hill occupy a very special place in my life and I want to share with you why. For one thing, I just liked to hang around the place. Looking back, I wouldn't deny for a moment that the red Coca-Cola soft drink chest and the candy case had a kind of magnetic effect upon me or that the whole place was just downright enchanting – its aromas were irresistible and there was something of interest to explore around every corner. Yet, as I look back, I believe something of a more enduring nature took place – a sense of validation was conveyed to me. In spite of getting in his way, breaking things and in general being a first class pain, my Uncle John Hill had a way of making me feel important. You see, he gave me the run of the whole place – behind the counters, behind the oak partition that separated the post office and bank from the rest of the store – he even allowed me to explore inside the walk-in vault – in my mind as a child, a kind of "Holy of holies" and I was allowed to enter!

Well, at the very end of my visit – the very last day, there came a crowning moment. Over the course of each summer I always managed to discover items in the store I felt I just had to have and at the top of my list this particular summer was a bone-handle pocketknife with three shiny blades. Now you have to understand that when an eight-year-old kid has been eyeing a particular pocketknife all summer long, the significance of that pocketknife gets magnified with each passing day. I mean to tell you, getting out of town with that pocketknife in your pocket comes about as close to being a "life or death" matter as you can get.

My Uncle John Hill was smart. He knew that if he gave me everything that caught my eye over the course of the summer he would end up giving half the store away. So, on the last day of my visit he would call me over, sit me down, and, face-to-face, we would have a pretty serious conversation. First, he would reach into his pocket and pull out the pocketknife that my eyes had been glued to all summer. Then, he would ask, "Is this the knife you are interested in?" Excited, I would answer, "Yeah, that's the one!" Then, as if he had not quite made up his mind, he would say, "Now, I don't know, this is an awfully expensive knife, it has a genuine bone handle and three good blades. Whoever owns this knife will need to take good care of it." I always felt that eventually I would get the knife, but Uncle John Hill had a way of stretching the process out – it seemed like an eternity before that pocket knife finally left John Hill's hand and found a new home in my pocket. Hesitating once more, he would add, "I need to think about this some more; you know, this is one of my very best knives – whoever I let have it will have to keep it clean and be careful with it. Knives can be dangerous, you know." "I promise I'll be careful and take good care of it." Finally, Uncle John Hill would say, "Well, as I said, this is one of my finest knives, but if you promise you will take care of it, I suppose I can let you have it." Then would come that transforming moment when the knife would actually pass from John Hill's hands into mine. To be sure, this little drama with all its suspense, would repeat itself for a number of summers, but as I departed for home I was convinced that I had the best uncle in the whole world and the finest pocketknife in the Western Hemisphere! Every kid ought to have an uncle with a general store!

A Pain in the Ass

Some days get off to a pretty bad start and turn out pretty good, and other days start out pretty good and turn out to be a pain in the ass! I want to tell you about a day that turned out to be a real pain in the ass! But, first, I want to say a few things about my Uncle John Hill.

Uncle John Hill was one of my favorite uncles, and I want to tell you, I had some good uncles. On the other hand, he was a pretty serious fellow who wouldn't put up with a lot of nonsense, and that caused a kinda problem since I hung around Uncle John Hill's general store a lot and that just naturally provided him with plenty of problems not to mention an endless supply of nonsense. Like the time I swiped a plug of Brown Mule chewing tobacco when I was about six years old and headed behind the store to have a chew. I think I coulda gotten away with it, except that instead of spitting I just swallowed the juice and nearly turned green before they found me. I know my Uncle John Hill loved me, but you have to understand, Uncle John Hill and Aunt Jessie didn't have any children, so they didn't always know quite what to do with me.

One day down at the Swords General Store, I overheard Uncle John Hill tell somebody that he had to go see a man about some cows he wanted to sell. Naturally, I asked if I could go with him. Knowing my reputation for getting into trouble, he was reluctant, but I kept after him till he finally gave in and said "OK." So off we went, me and Uncle John Hill in his old, black pickup truck headed for a pasture down on the Oconee River.

From the time we arrived things started going wrong. I hadn't taken ten steps before I managed to step in a fresh blob of cow manure, which to say the least, didn't set too well with Uncle John Hill. So, he asked me, "How in such a large pasture did you manage to step in the cow manure?" I didn't quite get the point of his question since I really hadn't given much thought to locating it – I just put my foot down and there it was! Now, there was an old empty sharecropper house on one side of the pasture. Uncle John Hill suggested that I go check the house out while he finished talking to the man about the cows.

So, I headed over to the sharecropper house where everything was fine until I slipped and managed to get a splinter in my rear. It wasn't an ordinary everyday splinter; it was huge! In fact, my rear end hurt so bad that I honestly didn't think I was long for this world. Naturally, I ran over to Uncle John Hill who was busy trying to strike a deal with the man about the cows. When he saw me crying and realized what had happened he assured me that he had "never heard of anyone dying from a splinter in their rear." By now, he was utterly frustrated with me, so he told me to go sit in the truck until he finished talking to the man about the cows and then we'd drive back to the store and he'd see what he could do. I knew he was pretty upset, so I did what he said do – went back to the truck and waited.

As we drove back to the store, it was so quiet you coulda heard a mouse pee on cotton. Uncle John Hill just looked straight ahead and didn't say a word – so, I figured I'd better not say anything either and I didn't. When we got back to the store, he told me to wait on the porch while he went inside, and that's just what I did. In a few minutes he came back with a big block of ice, and, in no uncertain terms, he told me to pull my pants down and sit on the ice. So, there I was, sitting on this block of ice on the porch of the Swords General Store with my pants pulled down for all the world to see. Everybody that went in and out of the store looked at me kinda funny-like, as if to say, why is John Walter sitting on that cold block of ice with his pants pulled down? Well, I didn't altogether know why I was sitting there myself! But, the one thing I did know was that my rear end was freezing!!

A few minutes later, Uncle John Hill came out on the porch with an old straight-back chair, which he sat down beside me and the block of ice, then he disappeared inside the store again. By this time my rear end was so numb from sitting on that block of ice that I couldn't feel a thing! The next time he came out he had an open pocketknife in his hand. At that point things began to happen real fast. First, he sat down in the chair beside me and the block of ice. Then he flipped me over his knee, and with everybody at the Swords General Store looking on, proceeded to do a little rural surgery on my rear end! To be honest, I did some world class kicking and screaming (not because it hurt – my rear end was too numb for me to feel anything) but, because I was scared!

As I said, it was just one of those days – the day started out pretty good, but turned out to be a pain in the ass – for both me and Uncle John Hill!

Decided Opinions

My Aunt Jessie not only had strong opinions, she also had "decided" opinions and her "decided" opinions were amongst her strongest held opinions. The way I got to know about Aunt Jessie's "decided" opinions was when she taught the older ladies Sunday school class at the Swords Methodist Church. Because she was so loud, you could hear her a mile away. You didn't have to listen very long before you would hear Aunt Jessie say to the ladies "Now, it's my "decided" opinion that . . . ," or "I'm of the "decided" opinion that . . ." and so on.

Aunt Jessie's "decided" opinions were like opinions that had been chiseled in granite. If you didn't know that Aunt Jessie was a devout Methodist, you might mistake her "decided" opinions for papal pronouncements. It was as if Aunt Jessie and God had gotten together and agreed to elevate Aunt Jessie's "decided" opinions to the status of Universal Truth, and knowing Aunt Jessie, I can't help believing that God might have been coerced in the process!

Well, it just so happened that one of Aunt Jessie's "decided" opinions was that a distinction should be made between "guilt feelings" and "outright guilt." To Aunt Jessie's way of thinking, guilt feelings could exist pretty much on the surface, like having a little dirt on you – something that would eventually either fall off or be washed away, but outright guilt was another matter. Outright guilt cut right down to your gizzard, and furthermore, too much outright guilt could tilt you in a downward direction and send you straight to Hell! Aunt Jessie's distinction between guilt feelings and outright guilt was not only worrisome, it could mess up an otherwise pretty successful day. You see, I had gotten pretty good at dealing with guilt feelings, but the way Aunt Jessie saw it, if I was actually guilty of doing something wrong, that was a different matter and could have some real worrisome consequences – and I want to tell you, I was getting "worrieda and worrieda" by the minute! As it happened, my discussion with Aunt Jessie about guilt feelings versus actually being guilty followed on the heels of something that happened down at Uncle John Hill's general store and that's what I want to tell you about.

When you entered Uncle John Hill's store, the first thing you saw was a red Coca- Cola soft drink chest and along side all kinds of other soft drinks in that red Coca-Cola chest was one called a Three Center. You don't have to be a financial genius to bring your pocket change up to the level of three cents and that's just what I set out to do. It took the better part of the morning, but I managed to put together three cents, which gave me honest access to the red Coca-Cola soft drink chest.

As I said, the first thing you saw when you walked through the door was the red Coca-Cola chest, but, if you looked to your right, there was a long counter and sitting on top of the counter was a long glass case divided into three sections.

The first section was for tobacco – all kinds – including Prince Albert pipe tobacco in a can. Uncle John Hill used to say, "Prince Albert must have been the most constipated man in the world cause he had been on the can since before the turn of the century." There was Sweet Peach snuff, even Brown Mule chewing tobacco that I learned the hard way, when you have a chew, you're supposed to spit, not swallow – just all kinds of good smelling tobacco. The last section of the glass case was for bread.

But, it was the middle section of the glass case, the section that had the letters C-A-N-D-Y on the front that grabbed my attention. As everybody knows, candy is good! It's just that simple. There, before my very eyes, were fourteen open boxes of penny candy. But, I had three problems. My first problem was that after paying for my Three Center soft drink, my pocket change had been reduced from three cents to zero. My second problem was that Uncle John Hill was very businesslike and knew exactly how much of everything he had in the store. My third problem was that I didn't have much experience as a thief, and therefore wasn't too sure of myself.

You see, I knew how to get my hands on the candy because Uncle John Hill allowed me to go behind the counter where the opening was, and since I was already committed to swiping it, my question was, did he know how many pieces of candy there were in a box? In other words, should I swipe a handful of candy from one box, or, take one piece of candy from each box. This took some pretty heavy thinking and my guilt feelings didn't make the process any lighter. I finally decided to swipe one piece from each box – that way he either wouldn't miss just one piece of candy or, maybe he'd figure he'd just miscounted how many pieces of candy were in each box to begin with. So, that's what I did. The first time Uncle John Hill went to the back of the store, I ran behind the counter and swiped one piece of candy from each box – about fourteen pieces in all!

I know I said I had three problems. But as the day wore on, I discovered I actually had a fourth problem. There I was, hiding behind Uncle John Hill's store with a pocket full of candy. At first, things were going all right, but gradually, things began to change. Guilt coated candy just doesn't taste as good as candy ought to taste. My problem was that I had a pocketful of perfectly good candy that didn't taste as good as it was supposed to, and that's when I headed down to Aunt Jessie's place in hopes of getting a little relief and salvaging what candy was left in my pocket.

Now I want to tell you, Aunt Jessie's distinction between "guilt feelings" and "outright guilt" has a lot of truth to it, but it can flat-dab ruin a pocketful of perfectly good candy – especially the part about your gizzard and sending you straight to Hell!